"9Marks, as a ministry, has taken basic biblical teaching about the church and put it into the hands of pastors. Bobby, by way of these study guides, has taken this teaching and delivered it to the person in the pew. I am unaware of any other tool that so thoroughly and practically helps Christians understand God's plan for the local church. I can't wait to use these studies in my own congregation."

Jeramie Rinne, Senior Pastor, South Shore Baptist Church, Hingham, Massachusetts

"Bobby Jamieson has done local church pastors an incredible service by writing these study guides. Clear, biblical, and practical, they introduce the biblical basis for a healthy church. But more importantly, they challenge and equip church members to be part of the process of improving their own church's health. The studies work for individual, small group, and larger group settings. I have used them for the last year at my own church and appreciate how easy they are to adapt to my own setting. I don't know of anything else like them. Highly recommended!"

Michael Lawrence, Senior Pastor, Hinson Baptist Church, *Biblical Theology in the Life of the Church*

"This is a Bible study that is actually rooted in the Bible and involves actual study. In the 9Marks Healthy Church Study Guides series a new standard has been set for personal theological discovery and corresponding personal application. Rich exposition, compelling questions, and clear syntheses combine to give a guided tour of ecclesiology—the theology of the church. I know of no better curriculum for generating understanding of and involvement in the church than this. It will be a welcome resource in our church for years to come."

Rick Holland, Senior Pastor, Mission Road Bible Church, Prairie Village, Kansas

"In America today we have the largest churches in the history of our nation, but the least amount of impact for Christ's kingdom. Slick marketing and finely polished vision statements are a foundation of sand. The 9Marks Healthy Church Study Guides series is a refreshing departure from church-growth materials, towards an in-depth study of God's Word that will equip God's people with his vision for his Church. These study guides will lead local congregations to abandon secular methodologies for church growth and instead rely on Christ's principles for developing healthy, God-honoring assemblies."

Carl J. Broggi, Senior Pastor, Community Bible Church, Beaufort, South Carolina; President, Search the Scriptures Radio Ministry

"Anyone who loves Jesus will love what Jesus loves. The Bible clearly teaches that Jesus loves the church. He knows about and cares for individual churches and wants them to be spiritually healthy and vibrant. Not only has Jesus laid down his life for the church but he has also given many instructions in his Word regarding how churches are to live and function in the world. This series of Bible studies by 9Marks shows how Scripture teaches these things. Any Christian who works through this curriculum, preferably with other believers, will be helped to see in fresh ways the wisdom, love, and power of God in establishing the church on earth. These s[   ]ractical, and accessible. I highly recommend this curriculum as [   ] embrace its calling to display the glory of God t[   ]

Thomas Ascol, Senior Pastor, Grace Bapti[ ] Executive Director, Founders Ministries

9MARKS HEALTHY CHURCH STUDY GUIDES

Built upon the Rock: The Church

Hearing God's Word: Expositional Preaching

The Whole Truth about God: Biblical Theology

God's Good News: The Gospel

Real Change: Conversion

Reaching the Lost: Evangelism

Committing to One Another: Church Membership

Guarding One Another: Church Discipline

Growing One Another: Discipleship in the Church

Leading One Another: Church Leadership

COMMITTING TO ONE ANOTHER: CHURCH MEMBERSHIP

Bobby Jamieson
Mark Dever, General Editor
Jonathan Leeman, Managing Editor

HEALTHY CHURCH STUDY GUIDES

:: CROSSWAY®

WHEATON, ILLINOIS

Committing to One Another: Church Membership

Copyright © 2012 by 9Marks

Published by Crossway
    1300 Crescent Street
    Wheaton, Illinois 60187

Cover design: Dual Identity inc.

First printing 2012

Printed in the United States of America

Trade paperback ISBN: 978-1-4335-2548-3
PDF ISBN: 978-1-4335-2549-0
Mobipocket ISBN: 978-1-4335-2550-6
ePub ISBN: 978-1-4335-2551-3

Crossway is a publishing ministry of Good News Publishers.

LB			26	25	24	23	22	21	20	19	18	17
16	15	14	13	12	11	10	9	8	7	6	5	

CONTENTS

INTRODUCTION

What does the local church mean to you?

Maybe you love your church. You love the people. You love the preaching, the singing. You can't wait to show up on Sunday, and you cherish fellowship with other church members throughout the week.

Maybe the church is just a place you show up to a couple times a month. You sneak in late, duck out early.

We at 9Marks are convinced that the local church is God's plan for displaying his glory to the nations. And we want to help you catch and live out that vision, together with your whole church.

The 9Marks Healthy Church Study Guides are a series of six- or seven-week studies on each of the "nine marks of a healthy church" plus one introductory study. These nine marks are the core convictions of our ministry. To provide a quick introduction to them, we've included a chapter from Mark Dever's book *What Is a Healthy Church?* with each study. We don't claim that these nine marks are the most important things about the church or the only important things about the church. But we do believe that they are biblical and therefore are helpful for churches.

So, in these studies, we're going to work through the biblical foundations and practical applications of each one. The ten studies are:

- *Built upon the Rock: The Church* (the introductory study)
- *Hearing God's Word: Expositional Preaching*
- *The Whole Truth about God: Biblical Theology*
- *God's Good News: The Gospel*
- *Real Change: Conversion*
- *Reaching the Lost: Evangelism*
- *Committing to One Another: Church Membership*

- *Guarding One Another: Church Discipline*
- *Growing One Another: Discipleship in the Church*
- *Leading One Another: Church Leadership*

Each session of these studies takes a close look at one or more passages of Scripture and considers how it applies to the life of the whole church. So, we hope that these studies are equally appropriate for Sunday school, small groups, and other contexts where a group of anywhere from two to two-hundred people can come together and discuss God's Word.

These studies are mainly driven by observation, interpretation, and application questions, so get ready to speak up! We also hope that these studies provide opportunities for people to reflect together on their experiences in the church, whatever those experiences may be.

Most people think church membership is like membership in a club. If you want a few extra benefits, or you aspire to be a leader someday, you should sign up. If not, you should feel free to come and go as you please. After all, church membership isn't in the Bible, is it?

What do you think? Is church membership biblical? Does it matter?

This study argues that church membership is biblical, that every Christian should be a member of a church, and that church membership makes a profound difference in the Christian life.

We begin with our need for church membership. Sin is deceitful, and we need to be truly accountable to others.

Next we consider the mandate for membership. After all, if church membership isn't biblical, it can't be anything more than optional. But we think that after carefully considering Scripture, you'll see that Jesus expects every Christian to be a committed member of a local church.

The next three sessions look at the goal, the challenges, and the nature of church membership. What are we working toward as church members? What are some of the roadblocks? And what exactly does it mean that we are members of one another?

The sixth session considers our responsibilities toward each other, and toward God, as church members. And the seventh session closes out our study by pulling back the curtain and glimpsing the glorious reality to which church membership points.

Whether you're a skeptic, ambivalent, or an active church member, we hope these studies will show you the necessity, power, and beauty of church membership.

AN IMPORTANT MARK OF A HEALTHY CHURCH: A BIBLICAL UNDERSTANDING OF MEMBERSHIP

BY MARK DEVER

(Originally published as chapter 10 of What Is a Healthy Church?*)*

Is church membership a biblical idea? In one sense, no. Open up the New Testament, and you won't find a story about, say, Priscilla and Aquila moving to the city of Rome, checking out one church, then another, and finally deciding to join a third. From what we can tell, nobody went "church shopping" because there was only one church in each community. In that sense, you won't find a list of church members in the New Testament.

But the churches of the New Testament apparently kept lists of people, such as the lists of widows supported by the church (1 Timothy 5). More significantly, a number of passages in the New Testament suggest that churches did have some way of delineating their members. They knew who belonged to their assemblies and who did not.

On one occasion, for instance, a man in the Corinthian church was living in immorality "that does not occur even among pagans" (1 Cor. 5:1 NIV). Paul wrote the Corinthians and told them to exclude this man from their assembly. Now stop and think about this. You cannot formally exclude someone if he is not formally included in the first place.

Paul appears to refer to this same man in his subsequent letter to the Corinthians by referring to the "punishment inflicted on him by the majority" (2 Cor. 2:6 NIV). Stop and think again. You can only have a "majority" if there is a defined group of people, in this case a defined church membership.

Paul cared "who was in" and "who was out." He cared because the Lord Jesus himself had granted churches the authority to draw a line—as best as they humanly can—around themselves, to mark themselves off from the world.

> Truly, I say to you, whatever you bind on earth shall be bound in heaven, and whatever you loose on earth shall be loosed in heaven. (Matt. 18:18; see also 16:19; John 20:23)

Healthy churches, we have said, are congregations that increasingly reflect the character of God. Therefore, we want our earthly records to approximate, as much as possible, heaven's own records—those names recorded in the Lamb's Book of Life (Phil. 4:3; Rev. 21:27).

A healthy church aspires to receive and to dismiss individuals professing faith, just as the New Testament authors instruct. That is, it aspires to have a biblical understanding of membership.

BIBLICAL MEMBERSHIP MEANS COMMITMENT

A temple has bricks. A flock has sheep. A vine has branches. And a body has members. In one sense, church membership begins when Christ saves us and makes us a member of his body. Yet his work must then be given expression in an actual local church. In that sense, church membership begins when we commit to a particular body. Being a Christian means being joined to a church.

Scripture therefore instructs us to assemble regularly so that we can regularly rejoice in our common hope and regularly spur one another on to love and good deeds (Heb. 10:23–25). Church membership is not simply a record of a box we once checked. It's not a sentimental feeling. It's not an expression of affection toward a familiar place. It's not an expression of loyalty or disloyalty toward parents. It should be the reflection of a living commitment, or it is worthless. Indeed, it's worse than worthless; it's dangerous, as we'll consider in a moment.

BIBLICAL MEMBERSHIP MEANS TAKING RESPONSIBILITY

The practice of church membership among Christians occurs when Christians grasp hold of each other in responsibility and love. By identifying ourselves with a particular local church, we are telling the church's pastors and other members not just that we commit to them, but that we commit to them in gathering, giving, prayer, and service. We are telling them to expect certain things from us and to hold us accountable if we don't follow through. Joining a church is an act of saying, "I am now your responsibility, and you are my responsibility." (Yes, this is countercultural. Even more, it's counter to our sinful natures.)

Biblical membership means taking responsibility. It comes from our mutual obligations as spelled out in all of Scripture's one-another passages—love one another, serve one another, encourage one another. All of these commands should be encapsulated in the covenant of a healthy church.

Church members will grow to recognize their mutual responsibilities the more they cherish the gospel, understand that conversion is God's work, and evangelize by instructing "seekers" to count the cost. Less will Christians regard their churches with a come-as-you-please and get-what-you-can attachment—one more store to peek your head into at the Christian mall or market. More will they view them as a body in which all parts care for one another—the home in which they live.

Sadly, it is not uncommon to find a big gap between the number of people officially on the membership rolls and the number who regularly attend. Imagine a church of three thousand members with only six hundred regularly attending. I fear that many evangelical pastors today might be more proud of their so-called membership than distressed by the large number of members not attending. According to one recent study, the typical Southern Baptist church has 233 members with only 70 attending on Sunday morning.

And is our giving any better? What congregations have budgets that equal—let alone exceed—10 percent of the combined annual incomes of their members?

Physical limitations can prevent attendance and financial burdens can prevent giving. But otherwise one wonders if churches are making idols out of numbers. Numerical figures can be idolized just as easily as carved figures—perhaps more easily. Yet God will assess our lives and weigh our work, I think, rather than count our numbers.

BIBLICAL MEMBERSHIP MEANS SALVATION AFFIRMATION

What's so dangerous about nonattending, responsibility-shirking members? Uninvolved members confuse both real members and non-Christians about what it means to be a Christian. And active members do the voluntarily inactive members no service when they allow them to remain members of the church, since membership is the church's corporate endorsement of a person's salvation. Did you catch that? By calling someone a member of your church, you are saying that that individual has your church's endorsement as a Christian.

So if a congregation has not set its eyes upon an individual for months, even years, how can it testify that that person is faithfully running the race? If an individual is missing in action but has not joined some other Bible-believing church, how do we know if he or she was ever really a part of us (see 1 John 2:19)? We don't necessarily know that such uninvolved people are not Christians; we simply can't affirm that they are. We don't have to tell the individual, "We know you're going to hell"; we only have to say, "We can no longer express our confidence that you're going to heaven." When a person is perpetually absent, a church endorsement is, at best, naïve; at worst, dishonest.

A church that practices biblical church membership does not require perfection of its members; it requires humility and honesty. It doesn't call them to bare decisions but to real discipleship. It doesn't discount the importance of an individual's own experiences with God, but neither does it assume too much of those not-yet-perfected individuals. This is why the New Testament presents a role for a corporate affirmation by those in covenant with God and with each other.

BIBLICAL MEMBERSHIP IS MEANINGFUL

I hope to see the membership statistics in churches become more and more meaningful so that the members in name become members in fact. From time to time, this means removing names from the church rolls (though not from our hearts). Most often, this means teaching new members what God intends for the church and continually reminding current members of their commitment to the life of the church. In my own church, we do this in a number of ways, from membership classes to reading the church covenant aloud every time we receive the Lord's Supper.

As our church has grown in healthiness, the head count on Sunday mornings has once again exceeded the number of names officially on our rolls. Surely this should be your desire for your church as well.

We don't love old friends well by allowing them to hold onto their membership in our congregations for sentimental reasons. We love them by encouraging them to join another church where they can love and be loved on a weekly, even daily, basis. In my own church's covenant, therefore, we pledge, "We will, when we move from this place, as soon as possible unite with some other church where we can carry out the spirit of this covenant and the principles of God's Word." This commitment is part of healthy discipleship, particularly in our transient age.

A recovered practice of careful church membership will have many benefits. It will make the witness of our churches to non-Christians more clear. It will make it harder for weaker sheep to stray from the fold and still call themselves sheep. It will help shape and focus the discipleship of more mature Christians. It will help church leaders know exactly for whom they are responsible. In all of this, God will be glorified.

Pray that church membership will come to mean more than it currently does. That way, we can better know whom to pray for and whom to encourage and challenge in the faith. Church membership means being incorporated in practical ways into the body of Christ. It means traveling together as aliens and strangers in this world as we head to our heavenly home. Certainly another mark of a healthy church is a biblical understanding of church membership.

WEEK 1
THE NEED FOR MEMBERSHIP

GETTING STARTED

1. Do you think it's important for Christians to be members of local churches? Why or why not?

MAIN IDEA

Christians need to be members of a local church so that, through a church's accountability and exhortation, we are protected from sin's deceiving, hardening effects.

DIGGING IN

Before we examine a passage of Scripture which shows us our need for church membership, let's clarify what exactly it is we mean by "church membership."

Here's how Jonathan Leeman defines church membership in his book *The Church and the Surprising Offense of God's Love*:

> Church membership is (1) a covenant of union between a particular church and a Christian, a covenant that consists of (2) the church's affirmation of the Christian's gospel profession, (3) the church's promise to give oversight to the Christian, and (4) the Christian's promise to gather with the church and submit to its oversight.[1]

Let's unpack these four elements a little bit:

1. **Church membership is a covenant**. That is, it's a solemn agreement between a Christian and a local church. In this covenant:
2. **The church affirms the Christian's profession of faith in Christ**. That is, by extending church membership to an individ-

---

[1]Jonathon Leeman, *The Church and the Surprising Offense of God's Love: Reintroducing the Doctrines of Church Membership and Discipline* (Wheaton, IL: Crossway, 2010), 217.

ual, the church is saying, "As far as we can tell, you're a Christian. We're putting our seal of approval on your claim to follow Christ."

3. **The church promises to oversee the Christian's discipleship.** This comes through teaching, preaching, the elders' oversight, and the mutual building up which all members of the church are to engage in (see Eph. 4:11–16).

4. **The Christian promises to regularly assemble with and submit to the church.** By committing to a church through membership, an individual Christian promises to regularly gather with this church and to submit to its authority and teaching.

1. Before we jump into the passage for this study, let's reflect a little on this understanding of church membership:

a) How does this definition differ from what you've thought or experienced of church membership?

b) Does this understanding of church membership make it more appealing to you or less? Why?

With this foundation in place, let's turn to Hebrews 3. The book of Hebrews is a "word of exhortation" (Heb. 13:22) addressed to professing Christians who are in danger of giving up their faith under the relentless pressure of persecution. In Hebrews chapter 3, the author specifically warns his readers not to be hardened by sin's deceitfulness:

[7] Therefore, as the Holy Spirit says,

"Today, if you hear his voice,
[8] do not harden your hearts as in the rebellion,
    on the day of testing in the wilderness,
[9] where your fathers put me to the test
    and saw my works for forty years.
[10] Therefore I was provoked with that generation,
and said, 'They always go astray in their heart;
    they have not known my ways.'
[11] As I swore in my wrath,
    'They shall not enter my rest.'"

[12] Take care, brothers, lest there be in any of you an evil, unbelieving heart, leading you to fall away from the living God. [13] But exhort one another every day, as long as it is called "today," that none of you may be hardened by the deceitfulness of sin. [14] For we have come to share in Christ, if indeed we hold our original confidence firm to the end. (Heb. 3:7–14)

Note: After the introductory remark, "Therefore, as the Holy Spirit says," verses 7 through 11 are an extended quotation from Psalm 95, which itself refers back to earlier incidents recorded in Exodus 17 and Numbers 14.

2. *What does the Holy Spirit exhort us not to do (vv. 7–8)? What does that mean?*

3. *What negative example does the author hold up for us? (Read Exodus 17:1–7 for background.)*

4. *What happened to the Israelites who hardened their hearts and disobeyed God (vv. 10–11)?*

5. *What does the author of Hebrews tell us to make sure* doesn't *happen to us (vv. 12–13)?*

6. *What does this passage tell us to do in order to make sure that we don't fall away from the living God (v. 13)?*

7. *Give some practical, everyday examples of how you exhort your fellow church members on a regular basis. If you can't think of any, what's one practical way you can begin to help others grow in godliness and not be hardened by sin's deceitfulness?*

8. *In verse 13, the author warns us not to be hardened by sin's deceitfulness. What does this teach us about sin?*

9. *Do you think of sin as something active, dangerous, and threatening, or merely as something that causes an occasional minor slip-up here and there?*

COMMITTING TO ONE ANOTHER

How should this passage's teaching about the nature of sin shape our lives as Christians?

10. How is someone who is not a member of a church especially susceptible to being hardened by sin's deceitfulness?

11. How do we know that we share in Christ (v. 14)? What effect should this have on how we live as Christians?

12. In light of this passage, how would you respond to someone who said, "I don't need to join a church. I can grow as a Christian just fine by coming to church whenever I want to, wherever I want to"?

WEEK 2
THE MANDATE FOR
MEMBERSHIP

GETTING STARTED

1. Are you a member of a church? Why or why not?

One reason some people don't join a church is because they think church membership is not in the New Testament. And some churches don't have formal membership because they don't see it in the New Testament.

This, then, is the million-dollar question. We can say all we want about the benefits of church membership, or our need for church membership, but we can only say that Christians must be members of local churches if that's what Scripture teaches.

So in this lesson we're going to consider the question, "Is church membership biblical?"

MAIN IDEA

Is church membership biblical? Yes!

We see church membership in a number of passages in the New Testament which teach that:

- Churches have an "inside" and an "outside."
- Church members are expected to know who does and does not belong to the church.
- Christians are under the authority of the church, such that if they persist in unrepentant sin, they are to be excluded from it.
- Christians are told to submit to their leaders, which means giving up our autonomy and putting ourselves under the church's authority.

- Leaders will give an account for those entrusted to their care, which means that they have to know who those people are.

DIGGING IN

In this study, it will be important to keep in mind our definition of church membership from the previous study:

> Church membership is a covenant (that is, a formal agreement) between a local church and a Christian in which the church affirms the Christian's profession of faith and promises to oversee the Christian's discipleship, and the Christian promises to gather with and submit to the church.

Thus, when we say, "Church membership is biblical," we don't claim to find an exact copy of any church's membership practices (which may include a membership class, an interview, and so on) in the New Testament. Rather, the New Testament clearly shows that churches are to have this kind of formal belonging and that all Christians are to commit themselves to local churches in this way.

1. Based on this definition of church membership, what power does a church have? That is, what "teeth" does it have for ensuring that members submit to the church? What consequences can it impose?

Does the New Testament Teach Church Membership?

Many people claim that church membership is not taught in the New Testament. So, we're going to test that claim by seeing how it stacks up to a few New Testament passages.

First, consider 1 Corinthians 5, a passage that is very important for our understanding and practice of church discipline. Paul writes,

> [1] It is actually reported that there is sexual immorality among you, and of a kind that is not tolerated even among pagans, for a man has his father's wife. [2] And you are arrogant! Ought you not rather to mourn? Let him who has done this be removed from among you.
>
> [3] For though absent in body, I am present in spirit; and as if present, I have already pronounced judgment on the one who did such a thing. [4] When you are assembled in the name of the Lord Jesus and

my spirit is present, with the power of our Lord Jesus, [5] you are to deliver this man to Satan for the destruction of the flesh, so that his spirit may be saved in the day of the Lord. (1 Cor. 5:1–5)

Then, after further urging the Corinthians to deal with this sin so that it doesn't spread through the church (vv. 6–8), Paul writes,

> [9] I wrote to you in my letter not to associate with sexually immoral people— [10] not at all meaning the sexually immoral of this world, or the greedy and swindlers, or idolaters, since then you would need to go out of the world. [11] But now I am writing to you not to associate with anyone who bears the name of brother if he is guilty of sexual immorality or greed, or is an idolater, reviler, drunkard, or swindler—not even to eat with such a one. [12] For what have I to do with judging outsiders? Is it not those inside the church whom you are to judge? [13] God judges those outside. "Purge the evil person from among you." (1 Cor. 5:9–13)

2. If the Corinthian church didn't practice church membership, could they exclude someone from their fellowship, as Paul instructs them to (vv. 4–5, 11–13; see also Matt. 18:15–20)? Keep in mind that Paul assumes that "outsiders" will be present in the church's meetings (1 Cor. 14:23–25).

3. Notice that Paul gives very different instructions about how the Corinthians are to treat those who are inside the church and those who are outside (vv. 9–13). If the Corinthian church didn't practice membership, how could they have known who was "inside" and who was "outside" the church?

4. What do you think? Did the Corinthian church practice church membership? Why or why not?

5. Based on this passage, do you think that churches should have membership today? Why or why not?

Let's consider another passage. In Hebrews 13:17, the author gives us very important teaching about how Christians are to relate to the leaders of their churches. He writes,

[17] Obey your leaders and submit to them, for they are keeping watch over your souls, as those who will have to give an account. Let them do this with joy and not with groaning, for that would be of no advantage to you.

6. Who does the author instruct Christians to submit to? Does this mean that all Christians must submit to all church leaders everywhere?

7. Imagine a situation in which an elder of a local church is faithfully preaching God's Word, and he confronts a sin in your life that you just don't want to address. How is this situation different for you if you're a member of the church versus a nonmember?

8. How would you summarize the relationship between membership and submission to the church's leaders? Can you truly submit to a church's leaders without joining the church?

9. Let's look at the question from another angle: Who are church leaders to give an account for? How are church leaders supposed to know who they are to give an account for?

As we've seen in these two passages, there is much New Testament evidence for the practice of church membership. We see church membership in the New Testament in that:

- Churches have an "inside" and an "outside" (1 Cor. 5:12).
- Christians are expected to know who does and does not belong to the church (1 Cor. 5:9–12).
- Christians are under the authority of the church, such that if they persist in unrepentant sin, they are to be excluded from it (1 Cor. 5:4–5, 13).
- Christians are told to submit to their leaders, which means giving up our autonomy and putting ourselves under the church's authority (Heb. 13:17).
- Leaders will give an account for those entrusted to their care, which means that they have to know who those people are (Heb. 13:17)!

10. Looking at all this biblical evidence together, would you say that local churches have an obligation to practice church membership? Why or why not?

11. In a similar vein, would you say that every Christian is biblically obligated to join a local church? Why or why not?

12. If a church does or doesn't practice church membership, how will that affect:

a) A church's attempts to practice church discipline?
b) The church's ability to hold each other accountable to live holy lives?
c) Leaders' relationships to those who are in the church?
d) The level of trust and depth of community that will develop in the church?

WEEK 3
THE GOAL OF MEMBERSHIP

GETTING STARTED

Many people think of church membership as simply putting your name on a list. If that's all it is, it's no wonder that they would be indifferent toward the idea. But based on our studies so far, a picture of church membership should be developing in our minds that is far more than having your name on a list.

1. What do you think are some of the ways that church membership should impact your life as a Christian?

MAIN IDEA

The goal of church membership is that every single church member would help the whole church grow to maturity in Christ.

DIGGING IN

In Ephesians 4, Paul exhorts us to live in unity in the church in light of the unity we have in Christ (vv. 1–6). Then, after explaining how Christ conquered death and gave gifts to his church (vv. 7–10), he specifically names some of those gifts and talks about the purpose for which Christ gave them:

> [11] And he gave the apostles, the prophets, the evangelists, the shepherds and teachers, [12] to equip the saints for the work of ministry, for building up the body of Christ, [13] until we all attain to the unity of the faith and of the knowledge of the Son of God, to mature manhood, to the measure of the stature of the fullness of Christ, [14] so that we may no longer be children, tossed to and fro by the waves and carried about by every wind of doctrine, by human cunning, by craftiness in deceitful schemes. [15] Rather, speaking the truth in love, we are to grow up in every way into him who is the head, into Christ, [16] from

whom the whole body, joined and held together by every joint with
which it is equipped, when each part is working properly, makes the
body grow so that it builds itself up in love. (Eph. 4:11–16)

1. *What are the gifts Christ has given to the church (v. 11)?*

2. *For what purpose did Christ give these gifts to the church (v. 12)?*

3. *According to this passage, who is it who does the work of ministry (v. 12)?
How is this different from the way we often think about "ministry" in the church?*

4. *What's the goal of the church's growth (v. 13)? What does this teach us about
how we should—or shouldn't—evaluate our church?*

5. *What threat to the church does Paul have in view in verse 14?*

6. *What does Paul say will happen once we all attain to mature manhood (v. 14)?*

7. *If maturity means that we are all unified in the truth and are able to successfully resist false teaching, what are some practical ways you can help others grow
toward that goal?*

8. *By what means does the church grow up to maturity (vv. 15–16)?*

9. *What does every member "speaking the truth in love" look like practically?
Where do these conversations occur?*

10. *What percentage of the body needs to contribute in order for it to grow properly (v. 16)?*

11. *What are some ways in which a biblical practice of church membership helps
contribute to the kind of growth this passage describes?*

12. *How would a church's growth in these ways be hindered if it didn't practice
membership?*

13. How do you think your contribution to the church's growth would be affected if you weren't a member of the church you regularly attend?

14. In light of this picture of every member of the body contributing to the body's growth:

    a) How would you describe the goal of church membership?
    b) What are some concrete steps you can take to help your church grow to maturity in Christ?

WEEK 4
THE CHALLENGES OF MEMBERSHIP

GETTING STARTED

1. What are some things that commonly cause friction or division between Christians?

2. Why do these things tend to separate Christians? What does it take to bring them back together?

MAIN IDEA

Every member of the church is called to overcome divisions and pursue unity in the church in order to reflect the church's union with Christ.

DIGGING IN

In 1 Corinthians 1:10–17, after encouraging the Corinthians based on the evidences of God's grace he saw in them, Paul begins to address an issue of utmost importance in the Corinthian church:

> [10] I appeal to you, brothers, by the name of our Lord Jesus Christ, that all of you agree, and that there be no divisions among you, but that you be united in the same mind and the same judgment. [11] For it has been reported to me by Chloe's people that there is quarreling among you, my brothers. [12] What I mean is that each one of you says, "I follow Paul," or "I follow Apollos," or "I follow Cephas," or "I follow Christ." [13] Is Christ divided? Was Paul crucified for you? Or were you baptized in the name of Paul? [14] I thank God that I baptized none of you except Crispus and Gaius, [15] so that no one may say that you were baptized in my name. [16] (I did baptize also the household of Stephanas. Beyond that, I do not know whether I baptized anyone

else.) [17] For Christ did not send me to baptize but to preach the gospel, and not with words of eloquent wisdom, lest the cross of Christ be emptied of its power. (1:10–17)

1. What does Paul appeal to the Corinthians to do (v. 10)?

2. How many ways does he state his appeal (v. 10)? What does this tell us about how important this issue of divisions in the church was to Paul?

3. What was reported to Paul about the Corinthian church (v. 11)? What specific examples of this does Paul give (v. 12)?

4. What attitude does the statement "I follow Paul" or "I follow Apollos" express? What's wrong with this attitude toward Christian leaders? (Hint: See verse 17 for one reason why the Corinthians may have been aligning themselves with some leaders over others.)

5. What's Paul's first response to these divisions in the church (v. 13)?

6. Why does Paul ask, "Is Christ divided?" What does this teach us about the nature of the church and why unity in the church is so important? (Hint: See also 1 Corinthians 12, especially verses 12 and 13.)

Just as Paul insists that the church must be united because it is the body of Christ, and Christ is not divided, so he reminds the Corinthians that it was not *Paul* who was crucified for them, and they were not baptized into the name of Paul (vv. 13–15). Rather, *Christ* was crucified for them, and they were baptized into *his* name. They belong to him, they are saved by him, they are one body in him, and so they should live in a way that expresses that unity.

7. The Corinthians were wrongly attaching themselves to one Christian leader or another at the expense of the church's unity. What are some of the right ways we should relate to leaders in the church? (See Phil. 1:15–18; 1 Thess. 5:12–13; Heb. 13:7, 17; 3 John 5–8)

8. How do these biblical ways of relating to local church leaders help build the church's unity?

9. What are some sources of division in the church that you've experienced? How do you think the apostle Paul would respond to each of these divisions?

10. What are some ways that you can seek to build unity in your local church? Give specific examples.

11. Think about the divisions we discussed in question 9. How does church membership help to foster unity in the face of these challenges?

WEEK 5
THE NATURE OF
MEMBERSHIP

GETTING STARTED

1. Have you ever been in a situation where you wanted to be included but you really weren't needed? How did you feel?

2. What are some ways that you depend on others in your daily life?

MAIN IDEA

The members of a local church are *interdependent*. We all need each other. No one should say that the church doesn't need them, and no one *can* say that they don't need other church members.

DIGGING IN

Sometimes people treat church membership as if it's just a formality: checking a box, putting your name on a list, and moving on. But the New Testament teaches that as members of the same church, we are members of a body, and we depend on one another just as much as a foot depends on an eye.

In 1 Corinthians 12, Paul begins discussing spiritual gifts, which the Corinthians had been using in selfish and self-serving ways. In the opening verses of the chapter Paul reminds them that all their different gifts are given by the same Spirit and for the common good (vv. 1–11). Then, in verses 12–27 Paul writes,

> ¹² For just as the body is one and has many members, and all the members of the body, though many, are one body, so it is with Christ. ¹³ For in one Spirit we were all baptized into one body—Jews or Greeks, slaves or free—and all were made to drink of one Spirit.

[14] For the body does not consist of one member but of many. [15] If the foot should say, "Because I am not a hand, I do not belong to the body," that would not make it any less a part of the body. [16] And if the ear should say, "Because I am not an eye, I do not belong to the body," that would not make it any less a part of the body. [17] If the whole body were an eye, where would be the sense of hearing? If the whole body were an ear, where would be the sense of smell? [18] But as it is, God arranged the members in the body, each one of them, as he chose. [19] If all were a single member, where would the body be? [20] As it is, there are many parts, yet one body.

[21] The eye cannot say to the hand, "I have no need of you," nor again the head to the feet, "I have no need of you." [22] On the contrary, the parts of the body that seem to be weaker are indispensable, [23] and on those parts of the body that we think less honorable we bestow the greater honor, and our unpresentable parts are treated with greater modesty, [24] which our more presentable parts do not require. But God has so composed the body, giving greater honor to the part that lacked it, [25] that there may be no division in the body, but that the members may have the same care for one another. [26] If one member suffers, all suffer together; if one member is honored, all rejoice together.

[27] Now you are the body of Christ and individually members of it. (12:12–27)

1. What metaphor does Paul use to describe the church in this passage?

2. What does Paul say is true of each of us who are Christians (v. 13)?

3. What does Paul say is not true of the body (v. 14)? What does this mean for the church?

4. What do the "foot" and the "ear" say in verses 15 and 16? What emotion or attitude is this expressing?

5. What are the two main points in Paul's response to what the "foot" and the "ear" say (vv. 17–20)?

6. Are you ever tempted to think that your church doesn't need you? Or have you ever interacted with someone who felt like the church didn't need them? How would you apply Paul's teaching here to that struggle?

7. In this passage Paul teaches that the body needs every member in order to be healthy (see the teaching in Ephesians 4:15–16). What are some concrete ways that you can use the gifts God has given you to build up your church?

8. What do the "eye" and the "head" say in verse 21? What attitude does this express?

9. What are the two main points in Paul's response to what the "eye" and "head" say in verse 21 (vv. 22–25)?

10. What are the two goals of God's arrangement of the members of the body that Paul mentions in verse 25? What is the example he gives in verse 26 to illustrate these things?

11. Can you give an encouraging example of some time you observed a member of your church mourning with another member who mourned? Of rejoicing with someone who was honored?

12. Are you ever tempted to think that you don't need the church—or at least that you don't need certain members of the church? How does Paul's teaching in this passage confront that attitude?

13. We could summarize this passage's teaching by saying that, as Christians and as members of local churches, we should think of ourselves less like independent individuals and more like members of a body. How should your interdependence with other church members impact:

   a) Who you talk to at church on Sunday morning?
   b) How you relate to church members who have a different ethnic background?
   c) How you relate to elderly/younger church members?
   d) Can you think of other concrete ways to apply this passage's teaching?

WEEK 6
THE DUTIES OF
MEMBERSHIP

GETTING STARTED

"Duty" sounds like a bad word today, or at least an unpleasant one. And it's true that some duties are unpleasant, or frustrating, or seemingly pointless.

1. What are some duties you'd really rather not have?

2. What are some duties that bring blessing and joy?

MAIN IDEA

As church members, we have the duty to imitate and submit to our leaders, to regularly assemble with the church, and to love and serve our fellow members. All of these duties are means by which we grow in godliness and help others to grow.

DIGGING IN

In previous generations, Christians have often drawn up lists of their duties as church members, both toward their leaders and toward each other.

That's what we're going to do in this study. We can't look at everything the New Testament teaches about our duties as church members, but we can cover some of the main points. We're going to look at three major passages in this study. To begin, let's read through them out loud.

> **Hebrews 13:7, 17:** ⁷ Remember your leaders, those who spoke to you the word of God. Consider the outcome of their way of life, and imitate their faith. . . . .¹⁷ Obey your leaders and submit to them, for

they are keeping watch over your souls, as those who will have to give an account. Let them do this with joy and not with groaning, for that would be of no advantage to you.

Hebrews 10:24–25: [24] And let us consider how to stir up one another to love and good works, [25] not neglecting to meet together, as is the habit of some, but encouraging one another, and all the more as you see the Day drawing near.

Romans 12:3–18: [3] For by the grace given to me I say to everyone among you not to think of himself more highly than he ought to think, but to think with sober judgment, each according to the measure of faith that God has assigned. [4] For as in one body we have many members, and the members do not all have the same function, [5] so we, though many, are one body in Christ, and individually members one of another. [6] Having gifts that differ according to the grace given to us, let us use them: if prophecy, in proportion to our faith; [7] if service, in our serving; the one who teaches, in his teaching; [8] the one who exhorts, in his exhortation; the one who contributes, in generosity; the one who leads, with zeal; the one who does acts of mercy, with cheerfulness.

[9] Let love be genuine. Abhor what is evil; hold fast to what is good. [10] Love one another with brotherly affection. Outdo one another in showing honor. [11] Do not be slothful in zeal, be fervent in spirit, serve the Lord. [12] Rejoice in hope, be patient in tribulation, be constant in prayer. [13] Contribute to the needs of the saints and seek to show hospitality.

[14] Bless those who persecute you; bless and do not curse them. [15] Rejoice with those who rejoice, weep with those who weep. [16] Live in harmony with one another. Do not be haughty, but associate with the lowly. Never be wise in your own sight. [17] Repay no one evil for evil, but give thought to do what is honorable in the sight of all. [18] If possible, so far as it depends on you, live peaceably with all.

Duty (verse #)	Toward leaders, other members, or God?	Reason/Motivation

List the Duties

First, go back through the passages and fill in *only* the left column of this chart, listing all the duties these passages lay on us as church members. (Some of these commands apply to how we relate to non-Christians; feel free to pass over those since in this study we're focusing on life within the church.)

1. Did anything on this list surprise you?

Duties toward Whom?

Next, go back through the list and write down whether each duty is toward church leaders, other church members, or God himself.

2. Are you surprised by how much the New Testament speaks of our duties toward our fellow church members? Why or why not?

Find the Motivation

Finally, read over just the passages from Hebrews and list the motivations the author gives for these duties. What reasons does he give for why we should do these things?

(If you want to do further study after this lesson, you can go through the rest of the duties you've listed and consider biblical motivations for them. Think especially about how what Jesus has done for us in his death and resurrection motivates us to love and serve our fellow Christians.)

3. What reasons did you list for each of the duties from Hebrews? Is there anything interesting or surprising about these?

Getting Specific

Having worked through this whole list of duties a few times, let's look a little closer at some of the specifics:

4. What are some ways that you already imitate your church leaders' way of life (Heb. 13:7)? What are some ways you can grow in imitating them?

5. What does submitting to and obeying your church's leaders look like in real life (Heb. 13:17)? Give some concrete examples.

6. Does the command to submit to and obey church leaders mean that they can command us to do whatever they want? Why or why not?

7. Have you ever considered that church attendance is a duty toward your fellow church members (Heb. 10:24–25)? Why is this the case? How should this impact what you do on Sunday morning?

8. Why is it important as church members not to think more highly of ourselves than we ought? What will happen if we do think of ourselves more highly than we ought?

9. Which do you think is harder:, to weep with those who weep or to rejoice with those who rejoice (Rom. 12:15)? Why?

10. Pick one of the duties we see in these passages and commit to prayerfully working on it for the next few weeks. What are some practical steps you can take to practice this?

WEEK 7
THE GLORY OF MEMBERSHIP

GETTING STARTED

Many Christians think of church membership as something dreary and dull. The word membership makes them think of long business meetings, working in the church nursery, sitting in church week after week, and other typical activities in the life of a church. And all this sounds more like meaningless rituals than deep spiritual experiences.

1. What are some aspects of church membership which can feel dull or dreary?

2. How do you find motivation to persevere in faithfully serving your local church?

MAIN IDEA

Church membership—and the activity of regularly assembling with the church which it entails—should offer a foretaste of the glory of heaven.

DIGGING IN

The book of Hebrews contains a long, detailed discussion of how Jesus's death and resurrection fulfills and therefore does away with the old covenant which God made with Israel through Moses. Toward the end of the book, the author presents a vivid contrast that illumines the practical difference between the old covenant and the new covenant:

> [18] For you have not come to what may be touched, a blazing fire and darkness and gloom and a tempest [19] and the sound of a trumpet and a voice whose words made the hearers beg that no further mes-

sages be spoken to them. [20] For they could not endure the order that was given, "If even a beast touches the mountain, it shall be stoned." [21] Indeed, so terrifying was the sight that Moses said, "I tremble with fear." [22] But you have come to Mount Zion and to the city of the living God, the heavenly Jerusalem, and to innumerable angels in festal gathering, [23] and to the assembly of the firstborn who are enrolled in heaven, and to God, the judge of all, and to the spirits of the righteous made perfect, [24] and to Jesus, the mediator of a new covenant, and to the sprinkled blood that speaks a better word than the blood of Abel. (Heb. 12:18–24)

1. What have we Christians not come to? List all seven things verses 18 and 19 describe.

2. What event in the Old Testament do verses 18 through 21 refer to? (See Exodus 19:16–25 and Deuteronomy 4:11–12 for background.)

3. What overall impression do verses 18–21 create? How would you feel if you were present at the scene it describes? (See especially verse 21.)

4. Why was it so terrifying for the Israelites to come face-to-face with God?

5. Verses 18 to 21, since they describe what it is like to come face-to-face with God's holy demands, also shed light on the plight of those who are outside of Christ. How should this fearful picture:

   a) Motivate our evangelism?
   b) Inform our evangelism?

6. What do verses 22 through 24 say that we Christians have come to? List every phrase below:

7. What does it mean that we have "come . . . to God" (v. 22–23)?

8. What has enabled us to come into a right relationship with God? (Hint: See verse 24.)

This passage describes the reality that we who are Christians have come into upon our conversion.

- We've come to God's holy city—that is, we are already members of his heavenly kingdom which will one day be fully manifested on the earth (v. 22).
- In this kingdom are angels who celebrate God's glory and believers who have gone before us and who are now glorified in heaven with God (v. 23).
- And we have come to God himself, the judge of all (v. 23), whom we need no longer fear because Jesus's blood speaks on our behalf (v. 24), so that God forgives our sins, counts us righteous in his sight, and accepts us as his children and heirs.

But this passage doesn't merely speak to these realities for us as individuals. Rather, the picture the author paints is of a heavenly *assembly*, of this whole multitude of believers gathered *together*, in perfect fellowship with God. Just as Israel assembled at Mount Sinai to receive God's law, so now the church already assembles around God's throne in heaven in anticipation of the final day when we will all dwell with God.

The New Testament portrays our present life in the church as a foretaste of this final, perfect assembly. Whenever the local church assembles, we experience a preview of the glory of the new heavens and earth. Thus, this passage teaches us not just about the glory of being a Christian, but about the glory of membership in the church, because it is in the assembly of the church that we experience the clearest foretaste of these heavenly realities. Our membership in the church is meant to be a pointer to our membership in God's heavenly assembly.

9. What are some ways in which your local church's regular gatherings are an anticipation of heaven?

10. Where are your thoughts tempted to wander to during your church's gatherings? How can this passage's teaching help you to engage in corporate worship wholeheartedly?

11. *Think back to the beginning of this study, when we discussed aspects of the life of the church that seem dreary and dull, and list them below. How does this passage's teaching help you approach each of those activities with a new mind-set?*

TEACHER'S NOTES FOR WEEK 1

DIGGING IN

1. Answers will vary.

2. In Hebrews 3:7–8, the Holy Spirit exhorts us not to harden our hearts. This means that we must not rebel against God and his Word, but rather must humbly submit to it. Rather than setting ourselves up against him, we must bow before him and allow his Word to expose our sin and lead us away from it (Heb. 4:12–13).

3. The negative example the author holds up for us is the Israelites' grumbling in the wilderness when they had no water (Ex. 17:1–7). In this incident, the people did not trust that God would be faithful to his word and would provide for them. Rather, as Psalm 95 says, they put God to the test and demanded that he give them what they wanted, now.

4. Hebrews 3:10–11 tells us that the Israelites who disobeyed God were punished by God and were forced to die in the wilderness instead of entering the Promised Land.

5. The author of Hebrews tells us to make sure that none of us have an evil, unbelieving heart which causes us to fall away from the living God (v. 12). Further, he warns us not to be hardened by sin's deceitfulness.

6. This passage tells us to *exhort each other every day* in order to make sure that we don't fall away from the living God (v. 13).

7. Answers will vary.

8. That verse 13 tells us not to be hardened by sin's deceitfulness teaches us that sin is an active, dangerous force within us. It teaches us that sin lies to us and seeks to entice us, promising things that it won't deliver. It teaches us that sin can "harden" us. It can lure us in to a life of greater and greater sinfulness until our hearts are no longer sensitive to God's Word and no longer convicted by his Spirit when we sin. In sum, verse 13 teaches us that sin is a deadly, dangerous enemy within us.

9. Answers to the first question will vary. Regarding the second question, the basic idea is that this passage's teaching about sin should stir us up to actively oppose sin, watch against sin, and make serious efforts to help others overcome sin. Rather than being passive and resting in a false sense of security from sin, we must help others overcome sin and seek help from

others to overcome sin because sin is constantly trying to deceive us. As John Owen famously put it, "You must always be killing sin or it will be killing you."

It should be emphasized that one of the author's main points is that we are not to engage in this effort alone, but we are to exhort *each other* so that we wouldn't be hardened by sin's deceitfulness. Because sin lies to us, we need others to help unmask those lies.

10. Someone who is not a member of a church is especially susceptible to being hardened by sin's deceitfulness because they are not accountable to anyone. Fellow church members are under the authority of the same church. They've committed to each other to watch over each other's lives. And, if a church member begins to cherish their sin more than Jesus, the whole church is called to pursue that individual, even to the point of exclusion from membership if he or she doesn't repent.

The problem with refusing to join a church is that you can simply walk away at any time with no real consequences. You don't have any real accountability. There's no "teeth" to the church's discipleship. And sin will exploit that to its advantage and our ruin. Further, the kind of independent, autonomous attitude which often leads to and is furthered by not joining a church is itself a dangerous manifestation of spiritual pride. It's like saying, "Yeah, other people might need help and accountability and exhortation in order to not be hardened by sin's deceitfulness, but not me!"

11. We know that we share in Christ *if we persevere to the end* (v. 14). Thus, perseverance in faith and faithful living is one of the great marks of being a true believer. This should encourage us to constantly renew our efforts to fight sin, strengthen faith, renew our love for the Lord, and seek to help and be helped by other believers. It should remind us that we're running a marathon, not a sprint, and that we need to constantly depend on God's grace in order to remain faithful to Christ throughout our lives.

12. Answers will vary, but they should especially draw on what we discussed in question 10. Further, consider the definition of church membership we discussed at the beginning of this session.

- If church membership involves the church affirming a Christian's profession, every Christian should desire that affirmation. Submitting ourselves to the church's examination should only help us to more clearly see God's work in our lives.
- Further, the church's promise to oversee one's discipleship means that the church is committing to do that individual spiritual good.

Not just me, myself, and I are trying to further my spiritual growth, but the whole church is striving to build me up in Christ.

- The Christian's promise to gather with the church and submit to its oversight is also spiritually beneficial. Gathering weekly with others gives them a chance to stir us up to love and good deeds (Heb. 10:24–25). Hearing Scripture read and preached, singing and praying together, and the other activities of corporate worship strengthen our faith and stir our souls. And submitting to the church's oversight helps us grow in humility—one of the very things a "Lone-Ranger Christian" lacks most.

TEACHER'S NOTES FOR WEEK 2

DIGGING IN

1. A church has the power of formal church discipline or excommunication, as we'll consider momentarily in 1 Corinthians 5 (see also Matt 18:15–20). That means it can remove its formal "affirmation" from someone who professes to be a Christian by removing the individual from its rolls and telling him or her to abstain from the Lord's Supper. The power of excommunication is the "teeth" given to the local church by Jesus in Matthew 18:17.

2. No. If the Corinthian church didn't practice church membership, Paul's instruction to them to exclude someone from their fellowship, to "purge the evil person from among you," would make no sense. If there's no means by which people are *included* in the church, there's no way for them to be *excluded*.

3. Again, if the Corinthian church didn't have church membership, there's no way they would have known who was "inside" or "outside" of the church. After all, church membership is simply a formal, public way of an individual committing to the church and the church committing to an individual. If there's no such thing as church membership, then there's no meaningful way to speak of the church having an "inside" and an "outside." But, as we see in these verses, not only did the Corinthian church have an inside and an outside, but Paul expected the church to *know* who belonged to the church and who didn't.

4. This question calls for personal reflection and response. Hopefully people will see that, given questions 1 and 2, it's quite clear that the Corinthian church practiced church membership.

5. Again, this question calls for personal reflection. The goal is for participants to understand that practicing church membership is the only way to be faithful to Paul's teaching in this passage. Since he instructs the Corinthians to exclude a radically immoral person, churches today should do the same. And since he instructs them to treat those who are inside the church differently from those who are outside the church, we are compelled to obey those same instructions. This means that our churches must practice membership.

6. The author tells his Christian readers to "submit to *your* leaders." While there is a sense in which Christians should respect all those who are true Christian leaders, Christians are not commanded to *submit* to all church leaders everywhere, but only to those leaders whom they have personally identified with through committing themselves to the church and submitting to the church's authority. In other words, Christians are to submit to those who lead the church they are a member of.

7. In a scenario in which a church elder is faithfully preaching God's Word and he confronts a sin in your life that you just don't want to address, if you're a nonmember, you can simply walk away with no strings attached and no real consequences. But if you've committed yourself to the church as a member, you have to address your sin. You can't simply run off to another church where they won't confront you, because the whole church has committed to holding you accountable to live according to the gospel, and you've submitted yourself to the church's oversight.

While this lack of freedom and autonomy seems scary, it's actually God's ordained means for helping us grow in godliness and overcome our sin. Remember our previous study? Sin is deceitful and hardening. That's why we need to be committed and accountable to a church, so that the church as a whole can expose our sin and keep us accountable to repent of it.

8. Basically, one aspect of becoming a member of the church is submitting to the church's leaders. That's what you're doing *by joining the church*. Whereas if you never join the church, by definition you are not submitting to its leaders.

While regularly attending nonmembers of a church may *choose* to submit to a church leader's teaching, in the most important way they are continually *not submitting* to them. By refusing to join the church, they're refusing to come under the church's, and its leaders', authority. Thus they are essentially retaining their autonomy, their authority over themselves. They may willingly submit to these leaders' teaching insofar as they like it and agree with it, but what happens if they hear something they don't like, something that hits a little too close to home? They can just get up and leave. Thus, in refusing to join the church, they are refusing to *obey Hebrews 13:17's command* to submit to your church's leaders.

9. Who are church leaders to give an account for? Those whose souls they *watch over*. If you wander into a church once in a while, aren't accountable to the church, and never commit yourself to the church, it would be quite a stretch to say that the church's leaders are *watching over you*.

How are the church leaders to know whom they are to give an account for? They are to give an account for those they watch over, that is, those who have committed to their oversight and entrusted themselves to their spiritual care through church membership.

Thus, it seems that this verse also indicates that the church the author of Hebrews was writing to practiced church membership. The leaders knew for whom they were to give an account, and the church members knew to whom they were to submit.

10. This requires personal thought and reflection, but the answer should be "yes" for all the reasons we've discussed.

11. The answer should be "yes" for all the reasons we've discussed. The Bible expects that:

- Churches will have an inside and an outside.
- Those inside the church are *Christians,* and those outside the church aren't.
- Christians will submit to the church's authority (such that they can even be excluded from the church if they don't repent).
- Christians are to submit to their leaders' authority.

For all of these reasons (and more) every Christian is biblically obligated to become a member of a local church.

12. Answers will vary, but here are some basic ideas:

a) A church will simply not be able to practice discipline because people are not "inside" the church, not under its authority, in the first place. On the other hand, practicing membership is a necessary first step toward a healthy practice of church discipline.

b) Because people have not committed themselves to the church, the church as a whole simply will not be able to hold people accountable to live as Christians. This will tend to undermine and take the "teeth" out of individual discipling relationships. On the other hand, practicing church membership means that every person who joins the church is committing to help the other members follow Christ.

c) Without church membership, church leaders don't have a clear sense of who they are accountable to watch over. With church membership, leaders more acutely feel the burden of caring for every sheep one by one.

d) In a church that doesn't practice membership, you're not really sure who's committed, who actually agrees with what the church believes, and so on. While Christians should seek to love and reach out to anyone who comes through the doors of the church, church membership fosters trust and deep community because church members are unified in the faith and have committed to each other.

TEACHER'S NOTES FOR WEEK 3

DIGGING IN

1. The gifts Christ has given to the church are apostles, prophets, evangelists, and the pastors and teachers (v. 11). While Christians disagree about precisely how to interpret the meaning of these titles, at the very least we can be sure that Christ still gives his churches pastors and teachers, since elders are to teach the Word (1 Tim. 3:2; Titus 1:9).

2. Christ gives these gifts to the church for the purpose of equipping the saints to do the work of ministry (v. 12).

3. According to this passage, it is the saints—all of them!—who do the work of ministry. This is different from the way we often think about "ministry" in the church because we tend to think that only the paid pastors do ministry, and we're the ones they minister to. According to Paul, pastors equip *us* to do the work of ministry, which means that our work in the church is far more important than we often think it is.

4. The goal of the church's growth is that every member would attain to the unity of the faith and of the knowledge of the Son of God, to mature manhood, to the measure of the stature of the fullness of Christ (v. 13). This teaches us that we should evaluate our church in terms of how well we are helping others grow in their knowledge of Christ, unity in the truth, and Christian maturity. Yet too often we evaluate our church based on whether we like the music on Sunday morning, whether the service is entertaining, whether we feel like the church meets our needs, and many other things. Rather, we should ask how *we* are doing, and how others are doing, in building up the whole body to a mature knowledge of Christ.

5. The threat to the church which Paul has in view in verse 14 is false teaching.

6. Paul says that, once we become mature, we will be able to successfully withstand false teachers. We won't be blown and tossed by winds of doctrine and we won't buy in to men's deceitful schemes (v. 14).

7. Answers will vary.

8. The church grows up to maturity as every member speaks the truth to each other in love and as every single member of the body supplies what it is supposed to in order to help the body grow (vv. 15–16).

9. Answers will vary.

10. One-hundred percent of the body is needed in order for the body of Christ to grow properly (v. 16).

11. There are a number of possible answers, including:

- It provides accountability which helps members to overcome sin and grow in holiness.
- Members' commitment to each other will lay the foundation for the kind of mutual upbuilding this passage describes.
- Church leaders' knowledge of whom they are accountable those for will help them shepherd and teach with greater personal knowledge of their flock and will help them equip every member of the church for ministry.

12. Again, there are a number of possible answers. Think about the opposite of the things listed in number 11.

13. Answers will vary, but participants should recognize that they will likely not have the same commitment to the church, accountability to the church, help from others, encouragement from others, and opportunities to minister to others if they do not join the church they attend.

14. In light of this picture of every member of the body contributing to the body's growth:

a) The goal of church membership is that every member would help the whole body grow to maturity in Christ.
b) Answers will vary.

TEACHER'S NOTES FOR WEEK 4

DIGGING IN

1. In verse 10, Paul appeals to the Corinthians to agree with each other, to do away with all divisions, and to be united in the same mind and judgment.

2. Paul states this appeal three different ways: "that all of you agree"; "that there be no divisions"; "that you be united in the same mind and the same judgment" (v. 10). This tells us that this is of utmost importance to him.

3. Paul has received reports that divisions exist in the Corinthian church (v. 11). Specifically, it has been reported to Paul that the Corinthians are identifying with certain teachers over against others, apparently forming factions in the church based on which teacher they liked best.

4. The attitude which the statement "I follow Paul" or "I follow Apollos" expresses is pride and exclusivism. This is not merely a loving affection for a leader, but is a divisive devotion to one leader as opposed to another leader and the Christians who follow him. What's wrong with this attitude is that it gives human leaders a kind of exclusive loyalty we should only give to God, and it results in divisions within the church. Further, based on Paul's veiled reference in verse 17, it seems that the Corinthians were attaching themselves to teachers not based on the soundness of their teaching (all the men Paul lists were sound teachers), but based on whose rhetorical style most pleased them.

5. Paul's very first response is to ask, "Is Christ divided?" (v. 13).

6. Paul asks, "Is Christ divided?" because he knows that the church is the body of Christ (1 Cor. 12:12–13). The church is intimately identified with Christ (Acts 9:4). Christ is *not* divided, and so the church shouldn't be either. This teaches us that unity in the church is important because it reflects the very unity of Christ and the unity we have with him and in him. The church's unity witnesses to the world about who Christ is.

7. According to the rest of the New Testament, we should:

- Respect and esteem our leaders (1 Thess. 5:12–13)
- Closely study their way of life and imitate their faith (Heb. 13:7)
- Submit to them in a way that makes it a joy for them to lead us (Heb. 13:17)

- Be prepared to rejoice whenever the gospel is preached, no matter who's preaching it (Phil. 1:15–18)
- Be prepared to sacrificially support all those who preach the true gospel, even if we have no personal connection to them (3 John 5–8)

8. These biblical ways of relating to local church leaders help build the church's unity because they lead us to submit to such leaders yet remember that that we ultimately are to submit to the Lord. Further, these biblical ways of relating to leaders teach us to respect and support all those who preach the true gospel (although we have a uniquely committed relationship to the leaders of *our* local church, as Hebrews 13 shows), rather than creating factions and divisions around personality or style. And within our own local church, we should submit to and respect all the leaders God has appointed, rather than playing one against the others.

9. Personal experiences of different sources of division in the church will vary. Components of the apostle Paul's response would include:

- How the church images Christ and the gospel
- Reflecting on the unity we have in Christ
- Allowing for liberty of conscience on matters that God's Word doesn't explicitly address (Romans 14; 1 Cor. 8–10)
- Urging us to pursue humility and consider others more important than ourselves (Phil. 2:1–11)

10. Answers will vary.

11. Here are several possible answers. Church membership fosters unity because:

- It ensures that all those who belong to the church have committed to the same faith.
- It creates a mutual commitment between everyone in the church— we can't just walk away when things get tough.
- It acts as a continual reminder of the unity we actually share as brothers and sisters in Christ.

TEACHER'S NOTES FOR WEEK 5

DIGGING IN

1. The metaphor Paul uses to describe the church in this passage is a body and its members.

2. Paul says that each of us who are Christians were baptized by the Spirit into the body of Christ (v. 13). This means that when we came to faith in Christ, we were united to Christ and to all those who are also united to him by faith. Our membership in a local church is the way we "put on" and the way we live out this unity we have with other Christians.

3. Paul says that the body does not consist of one member, but of many (v. 14). This means that the church is, and is meant to be, composed not of one kind of people who are all the same, but of people with different gifts, struggles, cultural backgrounds, and more. Just as there is unity in diversity among the members of a body, so there should be unity in diversity among the members of a church.

4. In verses 15 and 16, the foot and ear say, "Because I am not a ____ (hand/eye), I do not belong to the body." This expresses a feeling of inferiority, of not being needed, and of feeling excluded from the body.

5. The two main points in Paul's response are:

   1. It is the very nature of a body to have many members; if a body *didn't* have many different members it wouldn't be a body (vv. 17, 19–20).
   2. God is the one who has sovereignly determined how the body's members would be arranged (v. 18).

6–7. Answers will vary.

8. In verse 21, the "eye" and the "head" say "I have no need of you" to the other members of the body. This expresses self-sufficiency, independence, and perhaps even arrogance.

9. The two main points in Paul's response are:

   1. We treat the less honorable and presentable parts of our physical bodies with special honor, which means we should treat

> the "less honorable" members of the church with special honor (vv. 22–24a).
>
> 2. God has deliberately arranged the body this way, giving honor to the parts that lacked it, in order that the body would be unified and that the members would care for one another (vv. 24b–25).

10. The two goals of God's arrangement of the members (v. 25) are:

1. That there would be no division in the body.
2. That the members would have the same care for one another.

The example he gives in verse 26 is that if any member suffers, the other members suffer together with it, and if any member is honored, all the other members rejoice with it.

11–13. Answers will vary.

TEACHER'S NOTES FOR WEEK 6

DIGGING IN

Here is what the completed chart should look like. Each person's may look a little different depending on how they handle commands that overlap (such as "obey your leaders" and "submit to your leaders").

Duty (verse #)	Toward leaders, other members, or God?	Reason/Motivation
Remember our leaders (Heb. 13:7)	Leaders	
Imitate our leaders (Heb. 13:7)	Leaders	The "outcome of their way of life" is eternal blessing.
Obey our leaders (Heb. 13:17)	Leaders	
Submit to our leaders in a way that makes us a joy to serve (Heb. 13:17)	Leaders	To submit to our leaders is to our advantage.
Consider how to stir each other up to love and good works (Heb. 10:24)	Other members	
Not neglect meeting together, but instead regularly assembling with the church (Heb. 10:24)	Other members	
Encourage one another (Heb. 10:25)	Other members	The day of salvation and judgment is drawing nearer
Think of ourselves with humble, sober judgment (Rom. 12:3)	Other members	All of these commands in Romans 12 are grounded in "the mercies of God" by which Paul appeals to his readers (Rom. 12:1–2). "The mercies of God" refers to the gospel which Paul has expounded in the previous eleven chapters.
Use our gifts to serve others (Rom. 12:6)	Other members	
Genuinely love others with brotherly affection (Rom. 12:9–10)	Other members	
Outdo one another in showing honor (Rom. 12:10)	Other members	

Serve God diligently from the heart (Rom. 12:11)	God	
Rejoice in hope, be patient in tribulation, be constant in prayer (Rom. 12:12)	God	
Contribute to others' needs; show hospitality (Rom. 12:13)	Other members	
Rejoice with those who rejoice, weep with those who weep (Rom. 12:15)	Other members	
Live in harmony with other members (Rom. 12:16,18)	Other members	
Do not be proud, but associate with lowly people (Rom. 12:16)	Other members	
Do what is honorable in the sight of all (Rom. 12:17)	Other members	
Live peaceably with all (Rom. 12:8)	Other members	

The questions in this study are looking for personal reflections and practical application.

The only exception to this is question 6: "Does the command to submit to and obey church leaders mean that they can command us to do whatever they want? Why or why not?" The answer is that the command to submit to church leaders does *not* mean that they can command us to do whatever they want, because church leaders' authority extends only as far as they are faithfully teaching the Word of God.

TEACHER'S NOTES FOR WEEK 7

DIGGING IN

1. Verses 18 and 19 tell us that Christians have not come to:

    1. That which can be touched
    2. A blazing fire
    3. Darkness
    4. Gloom
    5. A tempest (that is, a violent storm)
    6. The sound of a trumpet
    7. A voice whose words made the hearers beg that no further messages be spoken to them

2. *Verses 18 through 21 refer to the time when God gave his law to the Israelites on Mount Sinai.*

3. *Verses 18 through 21 create the overall impression of terror, fear of judgment, and gloom.*

4. *It was so terrifying for the Israelites to come face-to-face with God because when their sin came up against God's holiness, God stood against them in judgment.*

5. *(a) The fearful picture verses 18 to 21 give us of the state of those who are outside of Christ should motivate our evangelism because we realize the depth of others' plight before God. And (b) it should inform our evangelism by helping us to clearly articulate the main problem non-Christians have, which is that God's wrath is against them because of their sin.*

6. Verses 22 through 24 say that we Christians have come to:

    - Mount Zion, *which is* the city of the living God, the heavenly Jerusalem
    - Innumerable angels in festal gathering

- The assembly of the firstborn who are enrolled in heaven
- God, the judge of all
- The spirits of the righteous made perfect
- Jesus, the mediator of a new covenant
- The sprinkled blood that speaks a better word than the blood of Abel

7. That we have "come . . . to God" (vv. 22–23) means that we have come into a personal relationship with him. Rather than being separated from him by our sin, we are now in fellowship with him.

8. What has enabled us to come into a right relationship with God is "the sprinkled blood" of Jesus Christ (v. 24), which "speaks" on our behalf—that is, it covers over our sins and brings us into fellowship with God through the new covenant.

9. *Answers will vary, but they should include:*

- In the church's corporate gatherings, we offer prayers to God together, but in heaven we will see him face-to-face.
- In corporate worship we sing praises to God, which we will do perfectly in heaven.
- The church is a holy people before the Lord, and we gather as a people who are distinct from the world. In heaven, God's people will be made perfectly pure.
- In the church's gatherings we hear God's Word preached and have our hearts stirred by the hope of the gospel; in heaven that hope will become a reality.
- In the Lord's Supper we proclaim Christ's death *until he comes*, at which time, Jesus tells us, we will feast with him in the great banquet of the kingdom of God.

10–11. Answers will vary.

Up-a-do Unlimited Presents:

Popular 8 Note So...

Music Patterns for Glockenspiel, Xylophone, Hand Bells and Piano

This book is for beginning musicians, parents, grandparents, teachers and all others who support and encourage the arts and music with special thanks to the Up-a-do Unlimited Crew — family and friends who also believe that every individual has unlimited potential.

Contents:

5-6-2018

Contents:

The Songs:

Greetings!

This book was created for you so that you can experience the life-changing joy that comes with making music! The crew at Up-a-do Unlimited designs Song Patterns for a precision-tuned Glockenspiel Xylophone so that new musicians of all ages, even those without the ability to read music, can have success playing an instrument.

This book can work with any tuned glockenspiel, xylophone, set of hand bells and even a piano. You can learn the songs in this book individually, or you can join in with your family, school class, or community group and make music together.

We would love to know how you are using your Popular 8 Note Song Book, and if you have any questions or comments, please let us know!

info@UpadoUnlimited.com

MUSIC EXTRA: There are free audio tracks of many songs on our website at www.UpadoUnlimited.com.

Beginnings

Starting a new activity - no matter what your age - takes courage, resources and support. In this book, Song Patterns for your instrument are provided to make it a little easier to take that first musical step. We encourage you to surround yourself with those who will help you learn, cheer your successes and perhaps even play along with you!

This book was designed to be used with instruments with eight notes in a C to C scale such as xylophones, glockenspiels, hand bells and piano. Sometimes instruments vary in their color scheme, but most are labeled with the letter of the notes. All of this book's song patterns are color-coded AND letter-coded, so as long as the instrument is marked with the letter of the notes, you can play along.

Some people use this book to help children who cannot yet read music play some tunes on the piano. They take pieces of easily removable white artist's tape, draw colored dots on the tape that match the colors in the song patterns, and then place these dotted tape pieces on the piano keys.

The Importance of Music

As soon as babies are able to hold an object, they start to bang and shake it, experiencing the joy of creating sounds. We never outgrow that delight in music, and although some people limit their enjoyment of music to just listening, a whole new world opens up when a person learns to play an instrument.

There are so many benefits to learning to play an instrument! It is well documented that learning to play a musical instrument stimulates multiple areas of the brain and increases the brain's cognitive ability, but it also does so much more.

Physically, playing an instrument enhances eye-hand coordination and balance. Academically, it can increase math ability and improve reading and comprehension skills as well as listening ability while sharpening concentration. Socially, playing together in a group boosts leadership and team work skills and also teaches discipline. Emotionally, music fosters self-expression, creates a sense of achievement, relieves stress, and promotes happiness.

Music Patterns

Many parents and classroom teachers feel unequipped to teach the next generation about music because they had little opportunity to learn themselves. Sometimes older adults who missed the chance to play an instrument when they were younger are determined to begin. Music therapists are often looking for tools to bring music to their patients. Children delight in banging the keys of a percussion instrument but need some help to know what to do next.

Yet, where does one who has not yet learned to read musical notation begin?

Most people can match colors or letters, which makes color and letter coded music song patterns a good place to start.

Many songs are easier than they first appear because sections of music often repeat. In some of the music patterns included in this book, the musician will play a couple of lines and then go back and repeat one of the earlier lines again.

Beat, Rhythm and Tone

Beat:

The basis of all music is the beat, that familiar steady thumping that everyone has in their own heartbeats. Beats are fragments of time that are all the same length. The beat can be fast or slow or somewhere in between. New musicians often need help maintaining a steady musical beat at first, and it can help to play along with a metronome. There are several free options online.

Rhythm:

After one learns to keep a steady beat, he or she can begin to experiment with rhythm. Rhythm is variable, and it determines the length of the notes. Music is divided into sections or measures, and many songs have four beats in every measure. In this book, the length of time to hold a beat can be determined by looking at the length of the color block. The longer the block, the more beats the note is held.

Many popular songs have four beats in every measure, and in most of the songs in this book, count 1-2-3-4, 1-2-3-4. "On Top of Old Smokey," "Pop Goes the Weasel" and "For He's a Jolly Good Fellow" will have three beats in every measure, and the count is 1-2-3, 1-2-3. Sometimes a song is a little more complicated and includes eighth notes. When this happens in a song with four beats per measure, count 1& 2& 3& 4&, giving the measure eight faster beats.

Tone:

Pitch or tone tells how low or high the note sounds to the ear. The lower notes will appear closer to the bottom of the song patterns, and the higher notes will be closer to the top. This book was created for the notes C D E F G A B C, with the Low C on the bottom of the music pattern and the High C at the top of the music pattern.

On the next page, the length of the rhythm boxes are shown with the number of beats that each type of box receives.

Music Notes and Rhythms

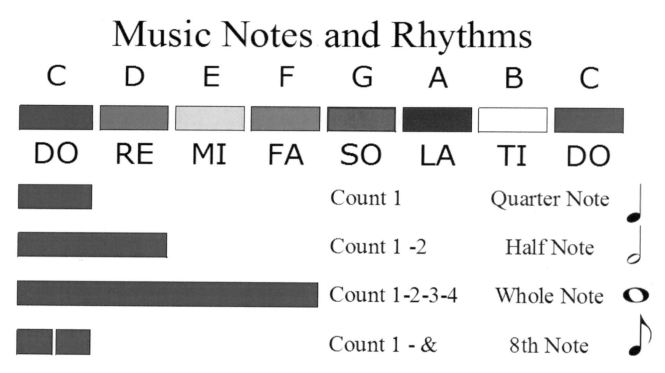

C   D   E   F   G   A   B   C

DO   RE   MI   FA   SO   LA   TI   DO

Count 1   Quarter Note

Count 1 -2   Half Note

Count 1-2-3-4   Whole Note

Count 1 - &   8th Note

Above are the lettered notes that make up an eight note scale.
In many songs, you count 1-2-3-4 for each section or measure.

Rounds and Duets

There is great satisfaction in playing a song on one's own, but it is an extraordinary experience when a musician plays that song with others. One of the best ways to begin making music in a group is to play or sing rounds. A round is a short song with two or more "voices" that can be played by instruments like a xylophone or glockenspiel, or it can be sung. Each musician plays the same song, but their start time is staggered. To play a round, everyone needs to first learn the song well, and then he or she is ready to join in with others.

The words to the rounds are included in this book, so one person can sing while another plays an instrument.

In a duet, one person plays the melody and a second person plays the harmony part. Again, it is important that musicians go over their individual parts first before combining it with others. But the teamwork skills gained as well as the satisfaction and self-confidence of knowing that one is able to hold a melodic part while combining it with others is well worth the effort.

Benefits for Classroom Teachers

We live in a time where budgets are tight and schools are reducing the amount of money they spend on the arts and music. Many elementary school teachers would like to introduce their students to the joy of music and help them reap the academic benefits as well, but most do not have a music background and do not know where to begin.

A frugal option for many schools is to purchase classroom sets of Glockenspiel Xylophones, and with a few simple Song Patterns, even teachers new to music training can have success. This is also a great option for those who want to bring music to summer camp and other community classes for students of all ages. To help school teachers and other community instructors get started, there are some classroom ideas at the end of this book.

Music can help with classroom management. When you create a musical environment in your classroom, it allows the shy children to join more comfortably in a group activity while teaching more aggressive children that they must learn to cooperate so they can participate. When children play music together, it gives all of the students a feeling of belonging.

Teaching students how to play a tuned Glockenspiel Xylophone allows teachers to reach children who learn best visually by having them look at the Song Patterns and match colors and letters. Kids who prefer to learn with auditory input can listen to their teacher and classmates play and hear the audio tracks of songs online. All young children learn by moving, and by its very nature playing a percussion instrument is a kinesthetic activity.

Playing music is very satisfying, and it is something students look forward to doing in their classrooms. It is sometimes easier to motivate students to get through some difficult academic tasks when they know that the reward is a chance to play their instrument. This works equally as well with homeschool students who need some encouragement to finish their studies.

To help parents, school teachers and other community instructors start teaching music with Glockenspiel Xylophones, there are some classroom ideas at the end of this book.

London Bridge

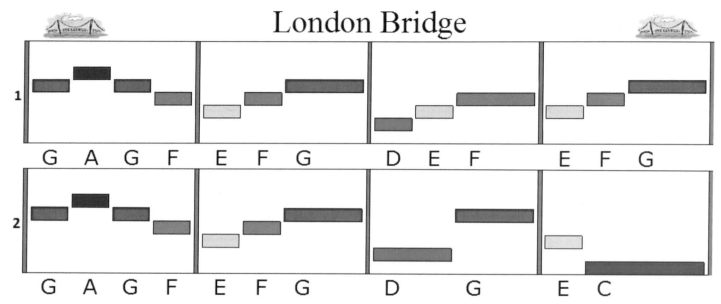

The letters on the song pattern above represent the notes on your instrument. You can match these letter notes to play the song, or if your instrument is color-coded in the same way as the chart on page 10, you can match the colors.

You can sing along as you play!

London Bridge is falling down, falling down, falling down.
London Bridge is falling down, my fair lady.

London Bridge Harmony

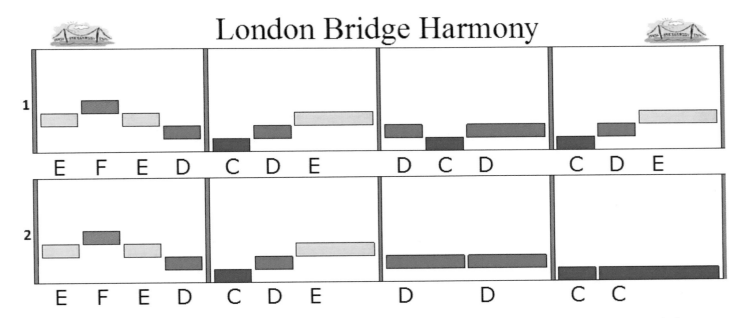

1

E F E D   C D E   D C D   C D E

2

E F E D   C D E   D   D   C   C

If you have two instruments, you can play a duet! It is important that both the musician playing the melody and the musician playing the harmony practice each piece separately before putting it together.

It is also helpful to have someone count the rhythm out loud or use a metronome. For this song, count 1-2-3-4, 1-2-3-4. The small colored blocks above get one count each. The larger "D" and "E" notes get two counts, and the very last "C" note of the song gets three counts.

London Bridge Advanced

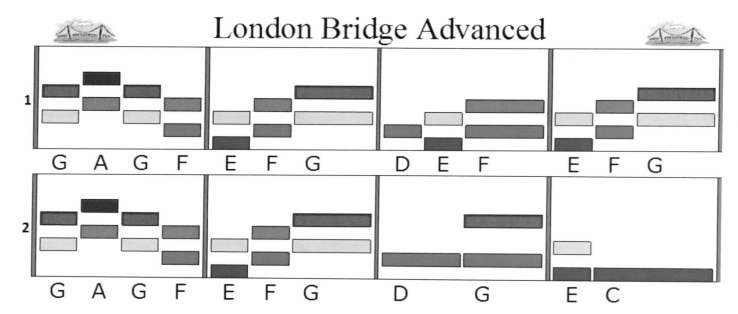

G A G F   E F G   D E F   E F G

G A G F   E F G   D   G   E C

The letters written above are the melody, and the extra blocks that are shown are the harmony. This is a blending of the melody and harmony of London Bridge.

If you are playing a glockenspiel or xylophone with two mallets, you can try holding one mallet in each hand and playing both the melody and harmony all on your own.

If you have color-coded keys on your piano, you can play both notes and create both the melody and harmony.

Mary Had a Little Lamb

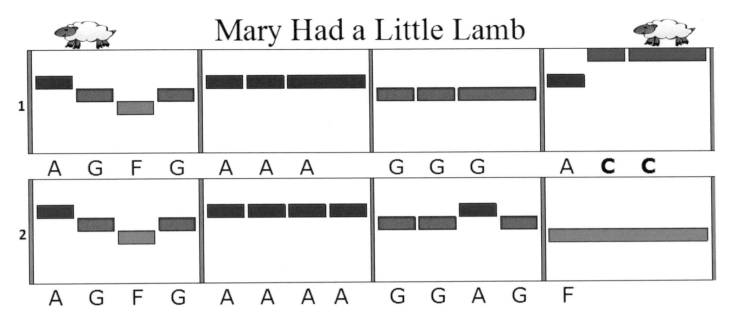

You will be playing the "High C" note in this song. See that the blue block is near the top and the letter "C" is darker.

You can sing along as you play! Play the song two times through!

Mary had a little lamb, little lamb, little lamb

Mary had a little lamb, its fleece was white as snow.

Everywhere that Mary went, Mary went, Mary went,

Every where that Mary went, the lamb was sure to go.

17

Row, Row, Row Your Boat

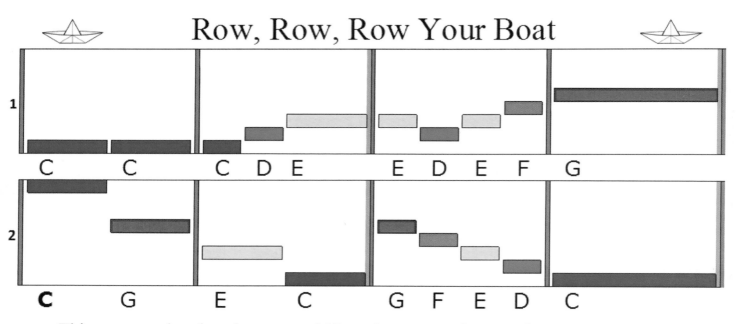

This song can be played as a round if you have more than one instrument. A new person can start the song when the first person crosses a pink line. Up to four people can play!

You can use two of the same instrument, or play two different instruments like a xylophone with a piano or a glockenspiel with hand bells.

Or you can sing! Row, row, row your boat, gently down the stream. Merrily, merrily, merrily merrily, life is but a dream.

The Paddle Song

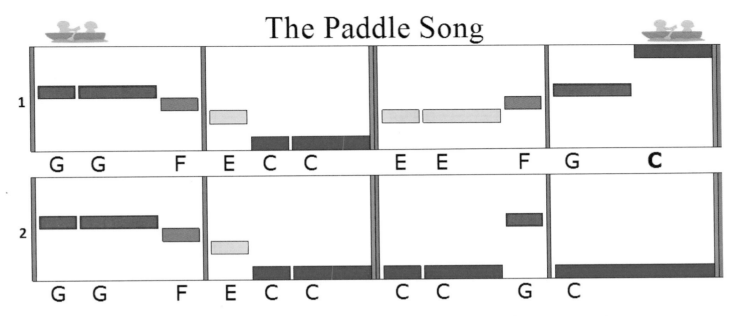

This song can be played as a round if you have more than one instrument. A new person can start the song when the first person crosses a pink line. Up to four people can play!

Or you can sing! Play the song two times through to sing both verses.

My paddle's clean and bright, flashing like silver,
Swift as the wild goose flies, dip, dip and swing.
Dip, dip and swing it back, flashing like silver,
Swift as the wild goose flies, dip, dip and swing.

I'm a Little Tea Pot

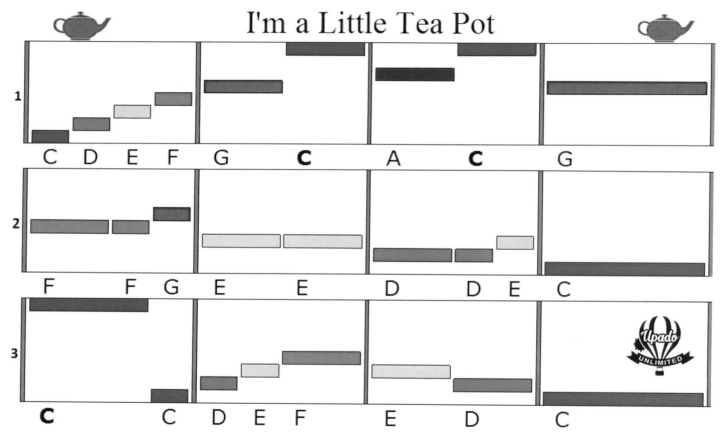

Songs have repeating patterns! This song repeats the first line half way through the song. **Here's what you do: Play Lines 1 and 2. Play Line 1 again, and then play Line 3.**

20

The Can Can

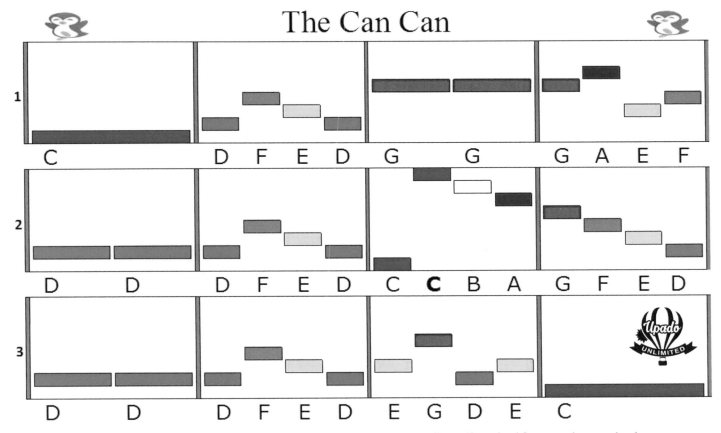

Songs have repeating patterns! This song repeats the first line half way through the song.
Here's what you do: Play Lines 1 and 2. Play Line 1 again, and then play Line 3.

Twinkle Twinkle Little Star

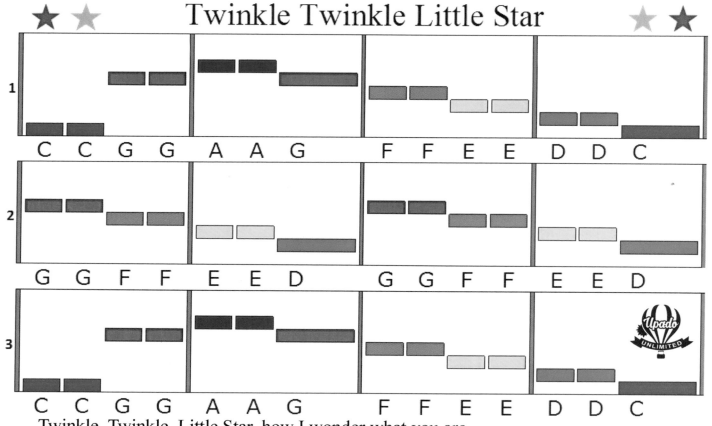

Twinkle, Twinkle, Little Star, how I wonder what you are.
Up above the world so high, like a diamond in the sky.
Twinkle, Twinkle Little Star, how I wonder what you are.

Harmony for Twinkle Little Star

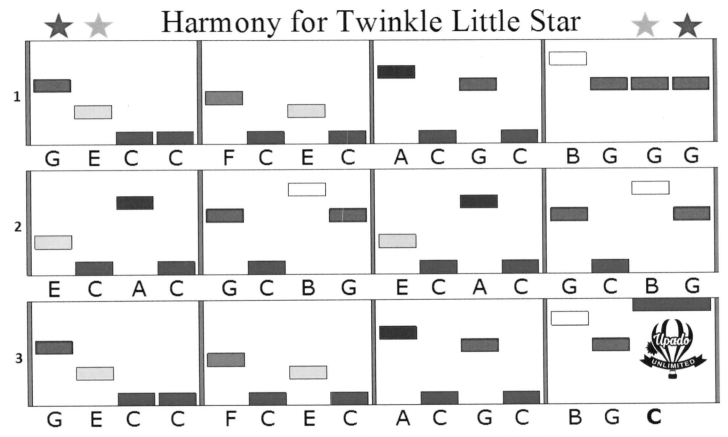

Here is a harmony piece you can try with Twinkle, Twinkle Little Star! If this is too difficult for you at first, you can play just the first block in each measure, giving the block 4 counts. To start, play "G" for four counts, then "F" for four counts.

23

Oh, Susanna

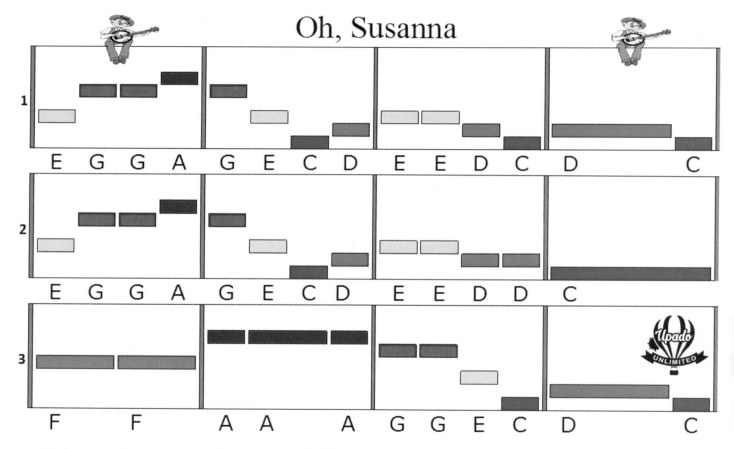

This song has a repeating pattern! Play Lines 1, 2 and 3 and then repeat Line 2.

24

Oh, Susanna Harmony

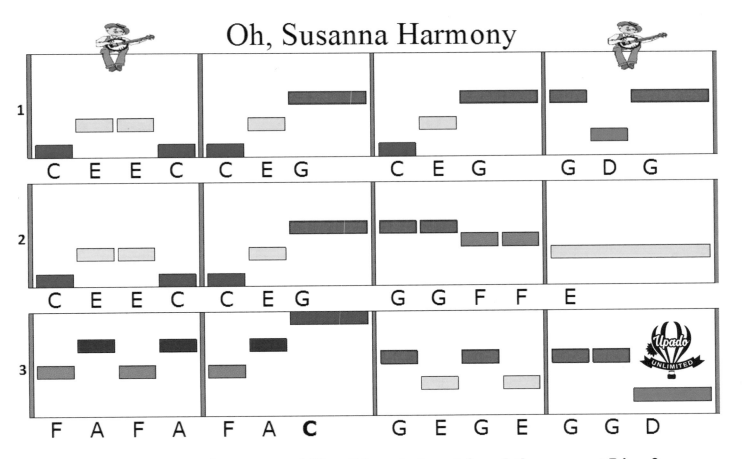

This song has a repeating pattern! Play Lines 1, 2 and 3 and then repeat Line 2.

Cripple Creek

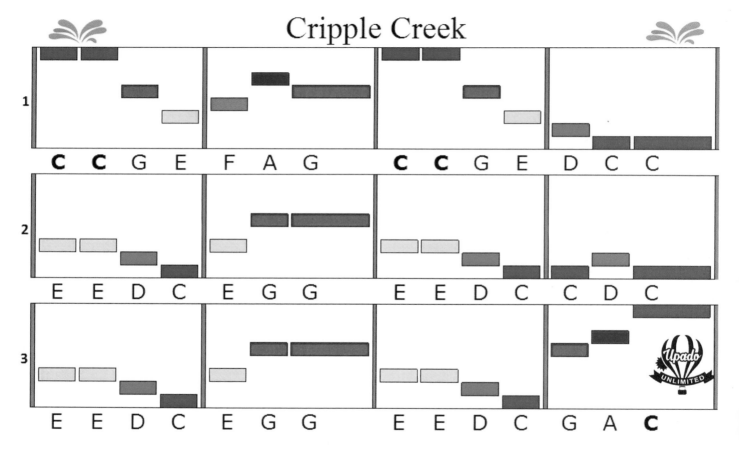

This song has a repeating pattern! Play Line 1 two times and then play Line 2 and then 3.

On Top of Old Smoky

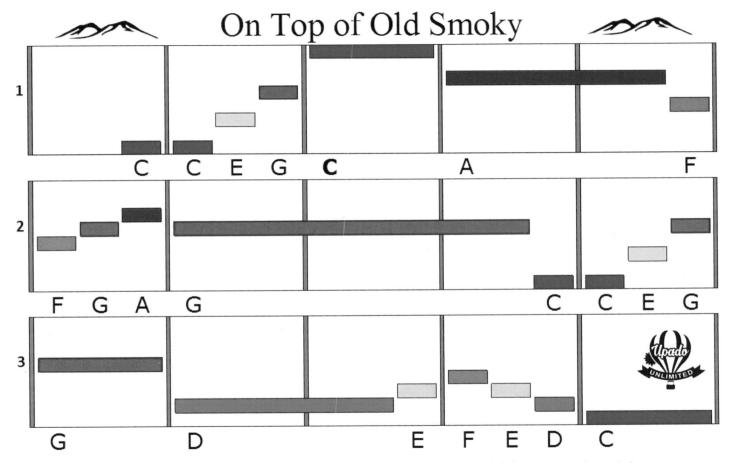

This song is in 3/4 time. Count 1-2-3, 1-2-3. Some notes are held for more than 3 beats.

Pop! Goes the Weasel

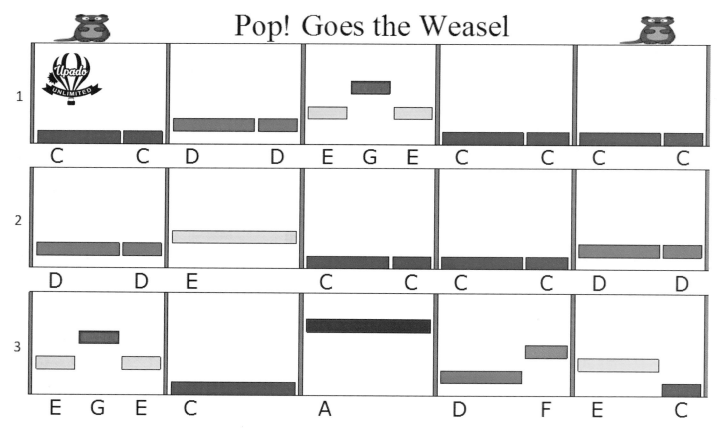

This song is in 3/4 time. Count 1-2-3, 1-2-3.

Sing: All around the cobbler's bench, the monkey chased the weasel.

The monkey thought 'twas all in fun, POP! goes the weasel!

Pop! Goes the Weasel Harmony

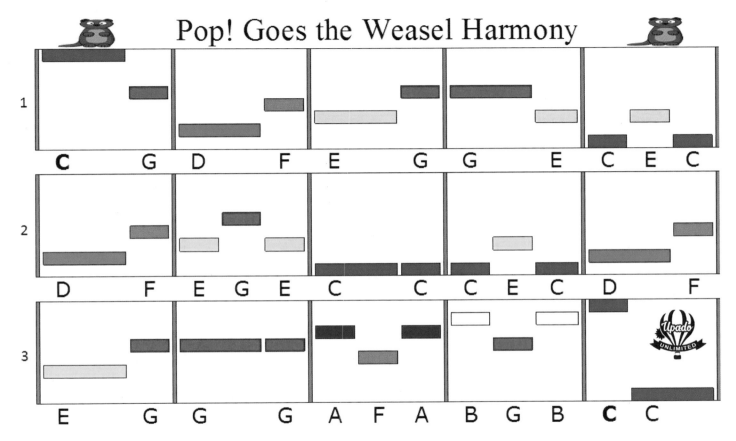

This song is in 3/4 time. Count 1-2-3, 1-2-3.

Pop! Goes the Weasel Part 2

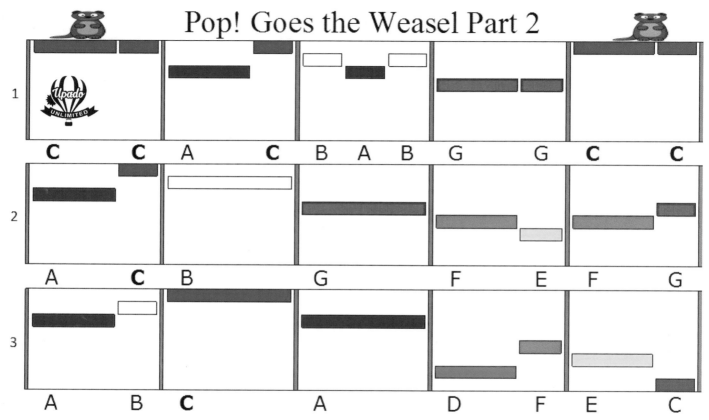

This song is in 3/4 time. Count 1-2-3, 1-2-3.

Sing: A penny for a spool of thread, A penny for a needle,

That's the way the money goes, POP! goes the weasel!

Pop! Goes the Weasel Part 2 Harmony

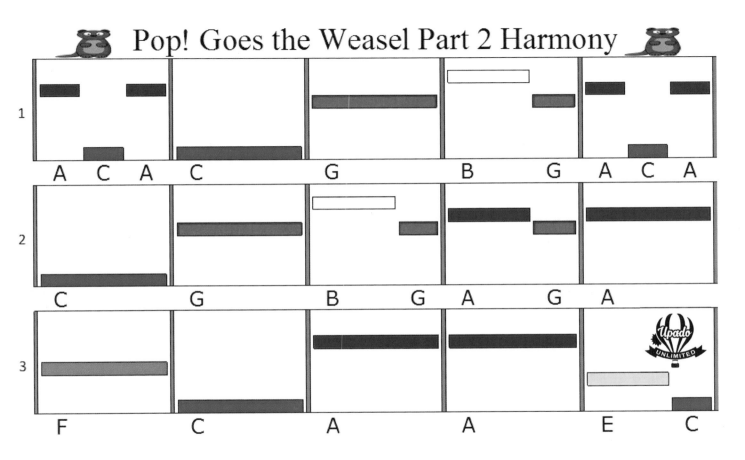

1   A   C   A   C   G   B   G   A   C   A

2   C   G   B   G   A   G   A

3   F   C   A   A   E   C

This song is in 3/4 time. Count 1-2-3, 1-2-3.

Beethoven's Ode to Joy

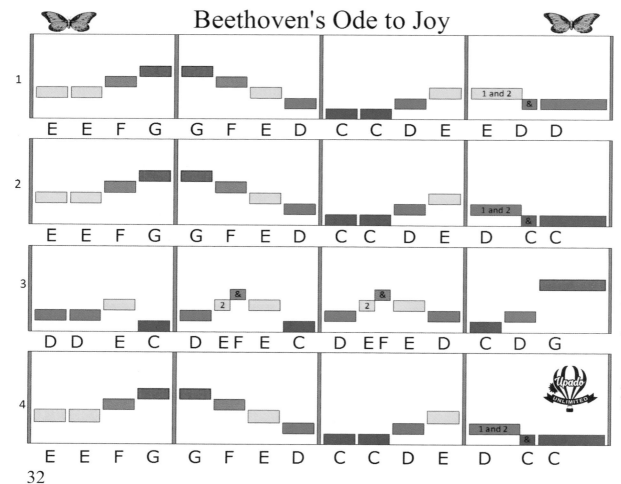

This song has 8th notes. Count 1& 2& 3& 4&.
There will be 8 beats in every measure.
The blocks that received one beat before now get two.

Beethoven's Ode to Joy Harmony

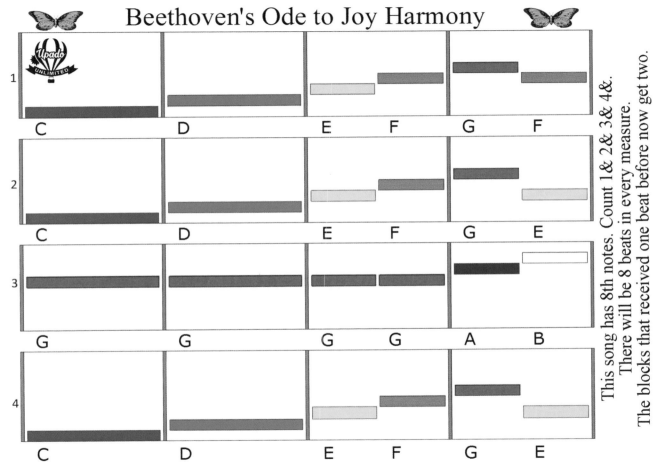

This song has 8th notes. Count 1& 2& 3& 4&.
There will be 8 beats in every measure.
The blocks that received one beat before now get two.

33

The William Tell Overture

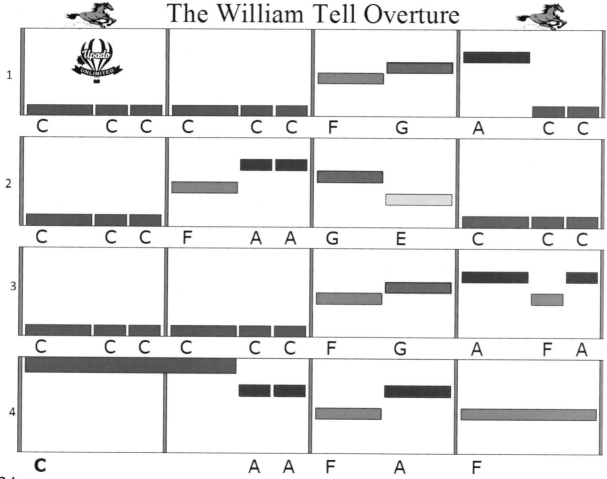

He's a Jolly Good Fellow

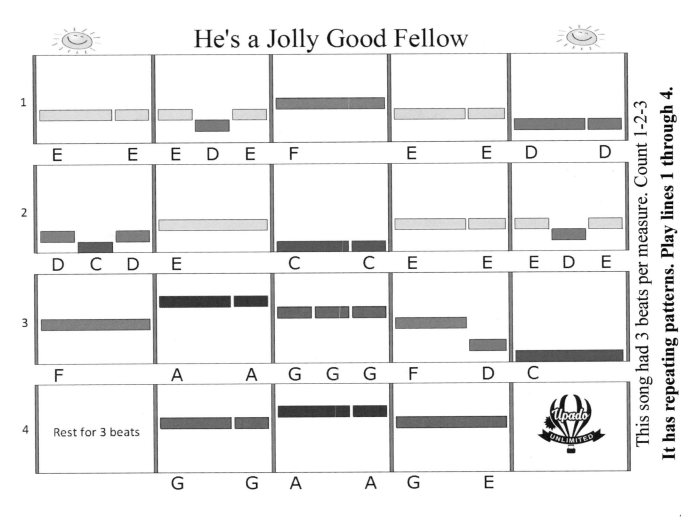

This song had 3 beats per measure. Count 1-2-3
It has repeating patterns. Play lines 1 through 4.
Repeat Line 4. Then play Lines 1 through 3.

35

Starting with the Beat

Facing a group of new musicians can feel like a daunting task, especially for a teacher with minimal music experience, but with some ideas to get everyone going, it can become a fun and successful experience.

If you are a teacher looking to introduce students to music with an eight note glockenspiel or xylophone, here are some ideas to help you get started.

Beat: The most crucial skill to teach at first is beat. You can help your students warm up their bodies and brains by having them stand and follow you as you tap different parts of your body or clap your hands. Because many of the songs in this book have four beats per section or measure, it is helpful to change your movement after every four beats. For example you can tap-tap-tap-tap (your head) and then clap-clap-clap-clap (your hands).

Metronome: A metronome is helpful and there are free options online. You can tap beats and play songs with a metronome ticking in the background keeping everyone together.

Instruments and Teachers

The Instrument: When it is time to hand out the Glockenspiel Xylophones to the class, make sure each student places the largest note to their left while the smallest note goes on the right. Mallets should be held loosely between the thumb and first finger so that the mallet bounces when it hits the metal key. This will cause the note to ring more clearly. The key should be struck near the middle for the best sound. Depending on the height of the desks and the size of the students, it may be easier for the students to stand while they play.

Teachers: Teachers who stand in front of the class will give their students an easier time if they play their Glockenspiel backwards with the small key to the left and the large key to the right so the students can follow the mirror image of what the teacher plays. For piano players in particular, this may feel awkward, so another option is to face away from the class, hold the instrument in the air in the left hand and have the students watch you play over your shoulder.

It is important to maintain control of the sound in your room. An easy way to get the students to stop playing is to have everyone hold their mallet in the air above their heads.

Finding the Notes

The Notes: Your students may want to play by hearing you call out the colors, or perhaps you will want to teach the students the names of the notes. The notes on the Glockenspiel Xylophones go from C to C – C,D,E,F,G,A,B,C. Most students who know their alphabet will be able to understand the order of the notes.

Find the Notes: Ask your students, "Can you find the green note and tap it?" When all the students are tapping on the green note, switch to another note. When the students are familiar with the location of the keys, you can begin to introduce a steady beat to the finding of the notes. If you call out red, then green and then yellow, the students can play red-red-red-red, green-green-green-green, yellow-yellow-yellow-yellow. You can change this by having them find the notes by the letter name instead. Because there are two "C" notes on a Glockenspiel Xylophone, you can call one "High C" and one "Low C" or call them "Big Blue" and "Small Blue."

You can then switch to having the students play the notes up and down the scale. Check everyone for proper instrument position and good mallet hold.

Activities to Get Started

The First Song: It is best to start with a song that most of the students know, like "Twinkle Twinkle Little Star" or "London Bridge." Having everyone sing the song together helps those who are not as familiar with the tune learn the notes and rhythms.

Follow the Leader: When it is time to play on the instruments, teachers can lead the students one note at a time. The teacher plays a note and then the students copy the teacher and play the same note. The teacher then plays the next note and the students mimic by playing that note. After everyone is comfortable with finding the notes on the instruments, you can play more quickly and with a steady beat.

Other Activities: Once a song is learned, there are new ways to play that you can try. Divide the class into 8 groups and give each group a note to play. Try and play one of the songs that the class has learned by having each group play on the note that they are assigned. This requires a lot of listening skills and cooperation. Another idea is to choose students to lead the group or conduct, allowing them to develop leadership skills.

Experiment with other activities and have fun!